AF478821

Title: **Cloudie Travels to Greece**

An educational series

Authors: **K.E. Manolas, Natasha Manolas, Katerina Manolas, Irene Fragaki**
Editing in Greek: **K.E. Manolas & Irene Fragaki**
Editing in English: **K.E. Manolas & Natasha Manolas**
Cloud creator: **Vivi Markatos**
Art Director/ Formatting: **Maria Stambouli**

© 2018 K.E. Manolas

Published by BookFairy Publications 2023.

 Ο Συννεφούλης Ταξιδεύει στην Ελλάδα - Cloudie travels to Greece
 Cloudiestravels@gmail.com

 www.bookfairypublications.com

More languages are available through the publisher.
Visit www.bookfairypublications.com for more information.

Cloudie Travels to Greece

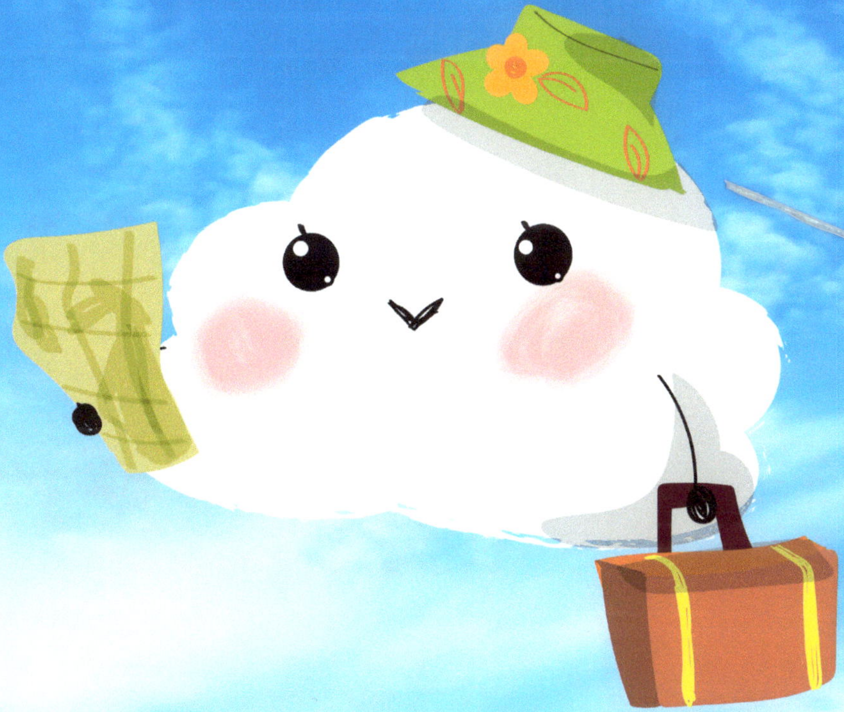

Once
upon a time,
there was a white, plump, and fluffy little cloud. He looked like a cotton ball and loved to spend his time playing in the sky. His name was Cloudie. He was playful and curious. Every chance he had, he asked as many questions as he could.

His dream was to travel around the world, get to visit many places, and make new friends. Just like that plane he saw traveling in the distance! However, he did not know how to begin his journey. Suddenly, he had an idea! He thought about asking Aeolus, the ruler of the winds, to help him. If Aeolus agreed to do so, the winds could carry him along their paths to many beautiful places. Feeling quite bashful, the little white cloud approached Aeolus.

Cloudie dared to say as he arrived in front of the king of the winds. Aeolus looked at him strangely. **"What do you need my help with?"** he abruptly asked.

the little cloud exclaimed with anticipation in his voice. **"So, you want to get to know the world..."** he began to say as he freed the North wind. **"North wind, push along our friend so he can get to know Greece."** Aeolus commanded the wind to glide the little cloud through the blue skies of Greece, the birthplace of democracy, as he handed Cloudie his sack.

"This sack contains all the winds. You must always keep it closed and never let all of them out at the same time. Remember this—you have to call the name of the wind that is out of the sack with you and tell him, "Go inside," before you can tell the next wind to exit by saying, "Come out." Aeolus also told the little cloud that it was essential for him to do as he was told, otherwise he would have a problem.

The little cloud was so excited that Aeolus had agreed to help him, that he quickly nodded "yes" to his instructions. However, he did not pay much attention to everything he was told.

The North wind feeling proud, as he was the first to show his new friend all the places he knew, built up momentum in the sky. They began their journey in **Northern Greece** by stopping on top of **Halkidiki**.

"**This is Halkidiki, and the three strips which look like legs are the three peninsulas that make up its land. Look closer at its eastern peninsula. Do you see the buildings on the rocks?**" asked the wind, as he gave the cloud a gentle push, so that he could get an even closer look.

"Yes, I see them!" Cloudie said with excitement.

"There, you can see **The Holy Mountain**, where more than twenty monasteries are built on rocks and steep slopes. This is where people praise and honor the **Christian Orthodox faith**, which is the religion of Greece."

Cloudie stood for a while in awe of the stone monasteries, which were on the cliffs of **Mount Athos**, before soaring away again in the beautiful Greek blue sky.

"What beautiful places! I want to see more!" he said with eagerness in his voice.

"Yes, but I am very tired now," whined the North wind. "You must let my brothers, the other winds, out of the sack, so they can help us."

"But Aeolus told me if I allow all of you to be out at the same time, you guys will cause chaos," he responded. "I can't disobey him!"

"**Nonsense! Aeolus likes to exaggerate in order to look wiser,**" assured the North wind playfully and continued, "**besides, my brothers know more places than I do. I promise you we will have a great time,**" the wind said with a crafty look.

Cloudie took some time to ponder in order to remember exactly what Aeolus had told him to do.

"What would the big deal be if I allowed more winds to accompany me? In fact, I believe it will be more fun that way, and they will take me to more places," he thought. After all, the North wind had been behaving perfectly.

So, he gave in to the wind's pleadings, opened the sack, and allowed the rest of them to come out. The winds stretched and began to blow joyfully in all directions, happy that they were set free.

''We are on top of **Macedonia**...

...the birthplace of **Alexander the Great**. Look down there! That is the **Star of Vergina**!'' Levante, one of the winds, exclaimed. Now Cloudie really believed that his decision to free them was the right one. This wind was already helping him learn more!

"What a beautiful star! What does it represent?" he curiously wanted to know.

''Tell me, how many rays do you see?'' Levante asked him.

"Sixteen rays!" Cloudie screamed out happily.

"Bravo! Sixteen. The four big ones represent the four elements—wind, water, fire, and earth. The other twelve rays symbolize the twelve Gods of Mount Olympus,'' answered the wind.

"Have you heard of the twelve gods of Olympus?" asked the North wind, taking Levante's place by pushing him away. Without waiting for an answer and with a soft breath blow, he directed Cloudie toward the tall mountain that was once the home of the twelve Gods.

This angered the rest of the winds because each one of them wanted to be the one to push him first. So, they started to blow fiercely, causing destructions on Earth. Cloudie, however, had already moved along, which prevented him from seeing what was going on.

"This is Mount Olympus!" the North wind told him, ignoring Levante and the South wind who were fighting.

"It is so tall! I can touch it!" Cloudie said ecstatically as he approached the tip of the mountain, touching it. It was so amazing for him to be able to feel the Earth. He watched people walking on it from up in the sky where he flew, and he wondered what it would be like if he could walk there too.

"Tell me, Northie, about the gods." Cloudie encouraged the North wind and smiled as he gave him a nickname.

"In ancient Greece, many, many years ago, it was believed that at the top of Mount Olympus, there lived twelve gods who were responsible for whatever happened to humans."

"So now the gods do not exist? Who were these gods?"
 "No, they do not exist anymore. Father of the gods was Zeus, and his wife was Hera. The other Gods were Poseidon, Demeter, Athena, Aphrodite, Apollo, Ares, Hermes, Artemis, Hephaestus, and Hestia."

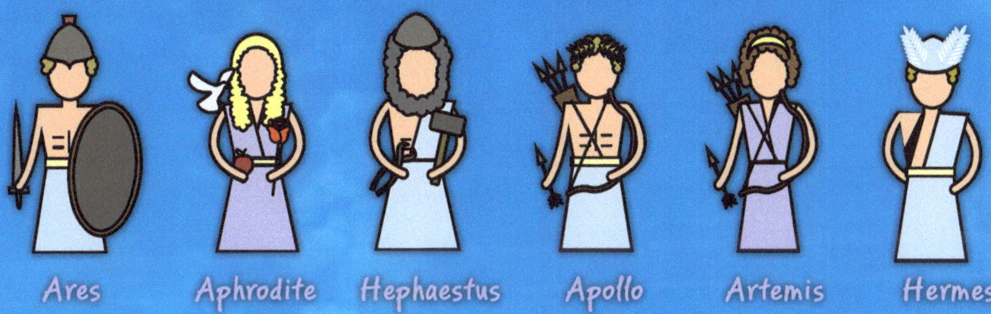

"Wow! All these gods helped people?" questioned Cloudie.
 "Most of them, yes, tried to help people," the North wind told him breathlessly, as he was tired from blowing his new friend around, and he stopped to rest.

At the same moment, **Levante** and the **South wind** appeared, and they continued to fight with all their strength over which place they should visit next. As soon as the **North wind** saw them blowing so hard, causing such dismantling, he tried to put some sense into them. All the while, **Pounente**, one of the other winds, crawled further away, feeling scared, leaving Cloudie all alone on the enormous mountain of Olympus.

The little cloud pulled himself to the side, as he was taken aback by the disaster the winds were causing at their passing. He saw trees uprooted, buildings trembling from the strong winds, and people holding on tight in order not to be blown away.

When the little cloud saw the winds drift far away from him, destroying everything in their path, he started to cry.

"What will I say to Aeolus now?" he mumbled inconsolably. How will I explain to him that I disobeyed him?" he said as he regretfully looked at the wind and added, "Oh, Northie, what have they done!" he cried terrified.

The wind, feeling just as responsible, went closer, risking being involved in the rival fight of the other winds.

"We made a mistake. We should have not disobeyed Aeolus. Don't worry, though, I will help you gather the winds again and, from now on, we will both be more careful. We won't do anything before we think of the consequences."

Cloudie promised, with tears in his eyes to Northie, that he would never disobey anyone's advice, especially when they are more knowledgeable and experienced than him. Look what had happened now! He was in the middle of nowhere and the winds had scattered all over the place.

"Don't cry! We will find them and put them back!" The
North wind reassured him as he gave him a soft push, which took him
above Delphi.

"Those ruins that you see down there comprise Delphi, the biggest oracle of ancient times," the wind told him, in an effort to cheer him up, as they continued their way to find the others.
"What is an oracle?"
puzzled Cloudie asked, looking down at the round-forming ruins.

''An oracle is a place where you go to find out about the future. The oracle of Delphi was visited by all the kings of ancient Greece when they wanted to find out if they would win the war or anything else that concerned them. In the oracle, there was a woman, Pythia was her name, who chewed bay leaves and said oracles. Oracle also means to give an answer to a question, like guessing what will happen.''

"Aww! I understand. Something may or may not happen," he said satisfied. "Could Pythia tell us if we will find the winds and if Aeolus will be mad at me because I disobeyed him?" he added innocently frowning.

The wind smiled. **"We will find them. I promise you we will!"** he assured his friend and gave him a push to move on.

Maistro, the calmest of the winds, suddenly took Cloudie out of Northie's stream and directed him towards **Athens, the capital of Greece**.

''**This is the Acropolis. The most important monument in Greece,**'' Maistro said, and immediately added, **"that big temple over there is the Parthenon. It was built in honor of the goddess Athena, protector of the city of Athens. Right next to it, there are six slender statues, the Caryatids."**

"Close to the rock that the Acropolis stands on is the ancient Agora, or market, which was a meeting place for many philosophers of ancient times. Across from the Acropolis, you can see Pnyx, the place where all of the important people of Athens, such as the politician Pericles, the colonel Themistocles, and the orator Demosthenes, used to stand to give their speeches.

"*Where will you take me to now?*" Cloudie asked, with an obviously curious look in his shiny eyes, as he had forgotten about the winds that had wandered away.

At that moment, **Graigos**, another wind, appeared and demanded to take Cloudie from **Maistro**'s current, so that he could drift him. Maistro had a non-hostile and quiet character and did not like to fight, so he let the cloud follow Graigos without any opposition.

"We are moving toward Peloponnesus, my little one"
Graigos informed Cloudie as he pushed to the southwest.
"Is it the one that looks like a hand?"

''Yes, it is. It is connected with the main land only through a small part of land, and it is separated by the Corinth Canal.''

Asclepius

The wind showed him **Epidaurus**, the home of **Asclepius**, the therapeutic doctor, as well as the ancient theater where, to this day, tragedies of **Aeschylus**, **Sophocles**, **Euripides**, and comedies of **Aristophanes** are still acted out. Then, they passed through Mycenae, which was the kingdom of Agamemnon, and the wind talked to him about the Mycenaean civilization.

Later, as they passed above the tips of Mount Parnon, also known as Malevos, the wind pointed down and said, "Look over there! That is **Sparta**. In ancient times, its king was **Leonidas**, who fought King Xerxes of Persia in the battle of Thermopylae. **Xerxes** had millions of men in his army, while Leonidas had only three hundred Spartans. Greeks were very robust soldiers."

Then, he showed him Mystras, a city full of castles, with the antiquated Byzantine churches and, with a little help from Northie, they continued their journey to the castle homes of Mani. On his left, Cloudie noticed a rock on which stood an impressive stone city surrounded by walls.

"What is this castle?"

"This is Monemvasia. It is a medieval town full of Byzantine churches. One of a kind in the whole world."

"How beautiful everything is!" Cloudie burst out, floating left and right, but he sensed a change in their direction.

He was not wrong. The strength of the North wind was beginning to fade as the other winds were approaching them, gusting all over the place. The little cloud felt petrified.

''We can't move on unless we show you this glorified place.'' Sirocco**, another wind, yelled as he was well caught up with them now, blowing so hard that Cloudie shook far away.

"Sirocco, take it easy! Don't puff that hard!'' Cloudie pleaded with him in order not to lose sight of the North wind, who had been the only one helping him.

"Ancient Olympia!" Sirocco continued unaffected, as if he had not heard a word that was said to him.

"And why is ancient Olympia so important?" dared to ask the curious cloud regaining his confidence.

"Because it was the most sacred place in Greece. It was devoted to the Father of the Gods. Do you remember what his name was?" asked Sirocco in an effort to test the little cloud.

"Zeus..." said Cloudie in a low uncertain voice.

"Great! Zeus! This is where the Olympic games, which take place every four years, even to this day, had begun. Back then, women were not allowed to take part in the Olympic games. Of course, this has changed now since the Olympics are a world class athletic event."

Cloudie carefully listened to Sirocco. However, at the same time, he looked for the North wind out of the corner of his eye. Once he spotted him, he silently pleaded with him for help with the other winds as he had promised.

The North wind began to blow slowly toward him as he yelled out, **"Remember the words! Remember the words!"**

As Aeolus has instructed him, the little cloud immediately started to shout out the names of the winds so he can get them back into the sack.

As each wind heard its name, it deflated and was pulled into the bag. Cloudie smiled, visibly relieved, as the winds bashed themselves unhappy with their entrapment.

"How about it now, should we continue our journey?" asked Sirocco who Cloudie had left out of the sack.

"Yes!" he exclaimed with relief that the winds were no longer causing chaos. So, they continued…

Their eyes became satiated by the green of the beautiful forest that adorned the mountains. And then, suddenly, in front of them, was blue.

"Ah! The sea! How beautiful it looks!" cried Cloudie, as he looked at the enchanting waters.

"You know, Greece has a lot of islands. More than two thousand altogether if you count them. But they are not all inhabited."

"Wow! Two thousand islands!" the cloud shouted.
"Yes, we won't be able to meet them all, but some of the larger ones are Crete, Rhodes, and Corfu," said Sirocco, pulling him toward the Ionian Sea.

The sack
of Aeolus

''Look! There is Corfu with the Achilleion Palace. It is the home of Queen Sisi, and it has a garden full of statues. A little further in the sea, you can spot Pontikonisi.''

As they finished their stroll on top of the **old city of Corfu**, it was time for Sirocco to return to the sack, giving way to Maistro. With a strong blow, Maistro took his friend toward the beautiful islands of Cyclades to show him Delos and Santorini.

The sack
of Aeolus

''We are on top of **Delos**, home of the god Apollo, with the very famous Avenue of the Lions. The temple of Isida is located here.

A little further down, you can see **Santorini**, known for its **volcano** that is still **active** to this day. I don't want to put down the rest of the islands, as each one has its own beauty, but I want you to see…

...**the sunset in Santorini**,'' Maistro said as he made a stop with his friend on top of **Oia**. He wanted him to see the sun making its dip in the deep blue waters, coloring them with the different shades of orange and red.

The sack
of Aeolus

"How much beauty can this country hide?" the cloud asked, as they watched the breathtaking dip of the life-giving sun.

"This country is not only beautiful but it has given the lights of civilization to the whole world. It has given birth to great philosophers, well known to the whole planet. Plato, Socrates, Aristotle and many more whose work they teach in all schools and universities around the world."

Cloudie could not hide the joy he felt that he had accomplished to see and learn all these important things about this country.

Their journey had to go on, though, as they had more to see. Maistro pushed the little cloud to the east towards the Aegean Sea, over the islands of Kos and Rhodes.

"**This is Kos, the home of Hippocrates. Hippocrates was the father of medicine. To this day, all doctors around the world, take his oath when they finish with their studies. It is called the Hippocratic Oath,**" the wind said as he shifted towards the biggest of the Dodecanese islands.

"There is **Rhodes**, the island of the sun. Look at its port and the two deer that stand there. There, once stood **Colossus**, one of the Seven Wonders of the World. He was so big and tall that ships passed through the opening of his legs. On the top of his head, he held a fire so ships could see the entrance to the port."

The sack
of Aeolus

The wind kept moving to show him the **Old Town** with the Castle of the Knights, the **Butterfly Valley**, and the picturesque village of **Lindos**.

"There is Karpathos! The second largest of the Dodecanese Islands which is located between Rhodes and Crete" the wind yelled out as he blew him in that direction.

"It is dreamlike!" his new friend said breathlessly.

"Her small villages look so beautiful."

"Here, you will see many traditional villages such as Pigadia, Volada, Aperi and the famous Olympos."

"That was the name of the mountain with the twelve Gods!"

"Ha!Ha!Ha!" The wind laughed out loud. **"Not Olympus, Cloudie. It's called Olympos. A Medieval Town which is the most beautiful in the Aegean! The people who live in this town still keep the customs and traditions of their ancestors. The villages of Karpathos are of the most beautiful and traditional villages in Greece."** explained Maistros.

Then, the wind **Graigos** took over once more.
''I will take you to the biggest and most southern island of Greece, Crete. People here talk with 'mantinades' when they are happy or when they are sad,'' the wind said.

"What are mantinades?" asked Cloudie curiously.

''They are words that come to their mind and they turn them into a verse.''

"Oh, like a poem."

''Good job! You are learning quickly! Look over there. These are the Cretan mountains. The White Mountains,

Ο σάκος
του αιόλου
The sack
of Aeolus

"Over here is Dikti. Do you know where it got its name from?" Cloudie looked at him strangely. How was it possible for him to know? *"No, I don't know but I would really like to learn!"* he said with excitement. **"Its name comes from mythology and it means the place where Zeus was born."**

"Look here too," the wind said as he blew to where he was pointing, **"on this very tall mountain called Psiloriti, it is said that Rea gave birth and hid Zeus without Kronos knowing. Zeus was raised by the Couretes and later on he was given to the Nymphs."**

That long line that you see is the Canyon of Samaria. People come from all over the world to walk through it.

Over there, is Knossos, with the well-known to everyone from mythology, Labyrinth. That was where King Minoas hid the Minotaur. A little further out is the city of Phaistos, which means glorious. It was there that the most known sample of hieroglyphic writing was found. The Phaistos disk, which is one of a kind. Knossos and Phaistos were the two largest towns in Crete at one point.''

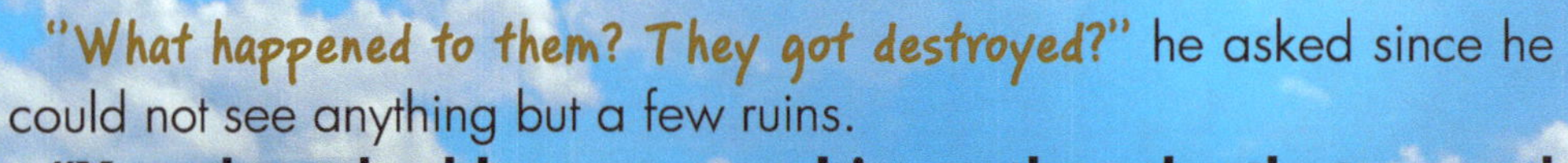

"**What happened to them? They got destroyed?**" he asked since he could not see anything but a few ruins.

"**Yes, there had been a very big earthquake that caused a big wave which covered and destroyed them,**" one of the winds in the sack yelled out to answer his question.

The sack
of Aeolus

Another wind rushed to say something before their journey came to an end. **"Look a little bit further, do you see that palm forest? That's Vai. The only natural forest in Europe which is so dense."**

"Wow! What magical picture!" exclaimed the little cloud with excitement.

The sack of Aeolus

"Everything is amazing! Thank you all so much. If I didn't have you accompany me, I wouldn't have seen nor learned so many things about Greece," the little cloud said as he put the last wind in the sack. It was time to return them to their king. It was getting late.

Aeolus smiled when he saw him coming from far away.

"Is everything ok? Did you get to see all the places and things you wanted to see?" he asked.

"I saw much more than I expected and learned a good lesson too. Thank you for helping me!" Cloudie told him as he laid the sack which held the winds in front of him.

"What lesson might that be?" Aeolus wondered.

"That you should always keep a promise and listen to someone more experienced when they give you advice. Not doing so might get you into trouble."

"Indeed, a valuable lesson you learned" Aeolus agreed not wanting to ask any more questions.

"Maybe after they rest a little, you could give them to me again so we can go on another trip," Cloudie requested feeling content from the exciting travels that he had just been on. He settled on the starry sky of Greece and started to talk to the shining moon about what he had learned until his eyes closed putting him in a deep sleep.

What is the name of the northern area of the Greece that is made up of three peninsulas?

Questions:

How many Gods lived at the top of Mount Olympus according to Greek mythology?

What is the capital of Greece?

Where did the Olympic games begin?

Who was the father of the gods?

What is the moral of the story?
What is an oracle?
Who was the King of Sparta?
Where is the Parthenon located?
Which Greek island was home to one of the seven wonders of the world?
Which is the biggest island in Greece?

Crossword

1) The ruler of the winds.
2) Who travels around Greece.
3) Has three peninsulas.
4) Birth place of Alexander the Great.
5) One of the twelve Gods of Olympus.
6) Delphi was the biggest one of ancient times.

7) One of the winds.
8) The King of Mycenae.
9) Medieval town full of Byzantine churches.
10) Home of Queen Sisi.
11) One of the seven wonders of the world.
12) Who was hidden by King Minoas in the Labyrinth?

Find the hidden words

Find the words across, down or diagonally.

KOS
PSILORITIS
KNOSSOS
LINDOS
SIROCCO

DELOS
SANTORINI
ISIDA
ZEUS
MYSTRA

THERMOPYLAE
EPIDAURUS
GREGALE
MANI

M	U	G	U	D	I	S	A	V	H	L	I	N	D	O	S	A	I	K	L
Y	A	D	Y	E	Z	G	J	D	S	A	Z	S	T	Z	X	T	Y	N	O
S	X	N	Y	L	A	K	O	S	Z	G	R	E	G	A	L	E	I	O	D
T	N	Y	I	O	J	L	J	E	P	I	D	A	U	R	U	S	S	S	F
R	R	M	P	S	I	L	O	R	I	T	I	N	U	S	P	Z	I	S	P
A	Z	J	M	X	B	R	S	A	N	T	O	R	I	N	I	U	D	O	A
T	H	E	R	M	O	P	Y	L	A	E	O	L	T	J	R	X	A	S	T
Z	M	J	B	Y	X	Y	S	I	R	O	C	C	O	R	J	H	I	N	H

Cloudcontest

Be part of Cloudie's Travels!

Write a story, no more than one page, about what adventure you would like to see Cloudie in, and which country you would like him to visit. Include a picture along with your paragraph.

On both write the following:

Name____

Age____

Address ______________________________________

Phone number__________________________________

Email_______________________________________

Email them to: **cloudiestravels@gmail.com**
On the subject line write: **Cloudcontest**

The story and picture that will be chosen by the authors will be used on the next Cloudie's Travels book and the lucky winner will get a free copy of the book.

Good luck!

The number of children can be adjusted depending on how many children you have.

Scene: A sunny day in the sky. Cloudie, a fluffy cloud, floats above Greece.

Narrator: Once upon a time, there was a plum-white cloud, fluffy like cotton wool, who liked to spend his time playing in the sky. They called him Cloudie. Cloudie was also very scandalous and curious. He wanted to know everything and asked as much as he could at every opportunity. He dreamed of traveling the world, seeing many places, and making new friends. But he needed to figure out where to start. So he thought of asking for the help of Aeolus, the guardian of the winds. If he agreed to help him, the winds would take him to many beautiful places. So, timidly and a little afraid, she approached him.

Cloudie: «Aeolus, I need your help.»
(Aeolus looks at him strangely)

Aeolus: «And what do you ask of me?»
Cloudie: «I want to explore the world!»
Aeolus: «So you want to know the world, my little one!»
(Cloudie nods «yes» and smiles)
Narrator: Aeolus, the king of the winds, gave him a sack and instructions on how to use it. So, our little cloud started its journey over Greece.

Cloudie: (singing):
I'm a cloud so light and free,
Traveling over land and sea.
Greece, oh Greece, so rich and grand.
Let's explore it hand in hand.
(Scene transition: Cloudie floats over the Dodecanese islands.)
The Dodecanese islands are each represented by children.

Cloudie: (excitedly):
 Dodecanese, islands so fair,
Children are playing everywhere.
Rhodes, Symi, oh so grand,
Let's make footprints in the sand.
(Children dance around Cloudie, representing different islands.)
Suddenly, Cloudie encounters the gentle wind, represented by a couple
of kids with flowing scarves.
Cloudie (curious):
Wind, dear friend, come help me soar,
Push me gently, I implore.
Through the islands, we will glide,
With your help, we'll be the guide.
(Wind children gently guide Cloudie over the islands.)

Cloudie: What is your name beautiful island?

Child 1 (Rhodes):
I'm Rhodes, with history so grand,
Knights and castles in the sand.
Come explore, hand in hand,
In my sunshine, you'll understand.

Cloudie: How about you? What is your name?

Child 2 (Symi):
Symi, with colors bright,
Harbors gleaming in the light.
Fishermen's tales, a joy to tell,
In my embrace, all is well.

Cloudie: You are both so pretty! Let me meet some others.
(Cloudie goes around to some of the islands, and the children introduce
themselves)

Child 3 (Kos):
Kos, where ancient ruins stand,
As if frozen in time's soft hand.
Biking through olive groves so green,
A paradise! It must be seen.
(Scene: The other four children step forward.)

Child 4 (Patmos):
Patmos, an island serene,
Where tranquility is ever seen.
In caves and monasteries old,
A story of faith and beauty told.

Child 5 (Kalymnos):
Kalymnos, climbers' delight,
Rocky cliffs, a stunning sight.
With courage high and spirits free,
Climbing to the sky with glee.

Cloudie: Oh, my goodness. You are so many!

Child 6 (Leros):
Leros, with bays so wide,
A peaceful haven where seas abide.
Calm and soothing, like a song,
In my embrace, you'll belong.

Child 7 (Karpathos):
Karpathos, wild and bold,
Legends and tales unfold.
Dances echoing through the night,
Underneath the starry light.
Finale:

(**Scene:** All children join hands, dancing in a circle.)

Children (singing):
Dodecanese, a delightful band,
Together, we've explored this land.
In the Aegean, under the sky so vast,
Our friendship will forever last.

Cloudie (gratefully):
Thank you, winds, for this grand tour,
Dodecanese, you've such allure.
Children, islands, hand in hand,
Together, we've explored this land.
(Children and Cloudie wave goodbye as the scene fades. Scene:
Cloudie floats away into the horizon.)

Cloudie (whispering):
Through the skies, we've had our fun,
Underneath the Grecian sun.
Clouds and children, a tale complete,
In the Dodecanese, where friendships meet.
(The curtain closes as the children wave at Cloudie disappearing into
the sky.)

K.E. Manolas (aka Connie) is an adult and children's book writer born and raised on the small island of Rhodes, Greece. She studied literature and creative writing at Rutgers University and worked as an ESL teacher for over ten years.

She is known for her imaginative and engaging stories that inspire children to use their creativity and explore their surroundings. In addition, her books often feature relatable characters and themes that resonate with young readers.

Children's books published in the US are "Your Pawprints Are On My Heart," available in several languages. «Cloudie Travels to Greece'', and «Cloudie Travels to Cyprus,» in English and Greek, which have received positive reviews from parents and educators, are now available globally.

Connie continues to write and publish children's books from her home in New Jersey, where she lives with her husband and two sons. She draws inspiration from everything around her and her birth island, which she visits yearly.

Katerina Manola grew up between Rhodes, where she was born, and the USA. She holds a Bachelor of Science in Biology (Rutgers, School of Environmental and Biological Sciences, The State University of NJ). She has extensive experience in public and private laboratories in Rhodes and as a science teaching assistant in the USA. In addition, she has been a member of a scientific team in local health institutions with several publications in medical and microbiological conferences. She holds an Advanced Diploma in Psychodynamic Psychotherapy from the Open European University and obtained her Master's Practitioner in Eating Disorders from the National Centre for Eating Disorders, UK. She also completed the CBT Applications - Cognitive Behavioral Therapy training course at the European Institute of Counseling and Psychotherapy (EICP). She holds a degree in Applied Psychology from the University of Derby (UK) and is also training in Systemic Psychotherapy at the Athens Center for the Study of Man (AKMA). Her involvement with creative writing led to several collaborative publishing projects aimed at adult and children's audiences.

Irene Frangaki was born and raised in Sitia, Crete, in 1976. She currently lives in Athens with her husband and five children. She is a descendant of the famous Cretan Vincenzo Cornaros from her mother's side. She writes adult novels, children's books, poetry, lyrics, and articles and enjoys drawing and making jewelry. She actively participates in the actions taken for the best living conditions of people with disabilities and their absolute acceptance by our society. Her works include: «The Secret of Happiness,» «The Butterfly of the Night,» «The Star and the Wish,» and «White Dreams.» She participated collectively in the projects «Cloudy Travels to Greece,» & «Cloudy Travels to Cyprus,» «127 Voices of the Soul,» & «The Christmas novel of… 17».

Natasha Manolas was born in New Jersey. She received a Bachelor of Arts degree in Psychology from The College of New Jersey. Natasha continued her education to receive a Master of Arts degree in Educational Psychology and a Post-Masters Professional Diploma from Kean University in School Psychology. She is a licensed school psychologist in the state of New Jersey, where she currently resides. Natasha has a passion for the interrelated worlds of psychology and education. She is a first-generation Greek American. This is her first children's book.

More books from BookFairy Publications

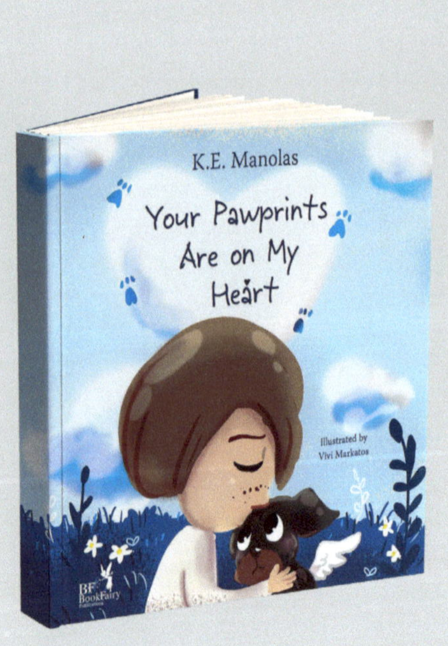

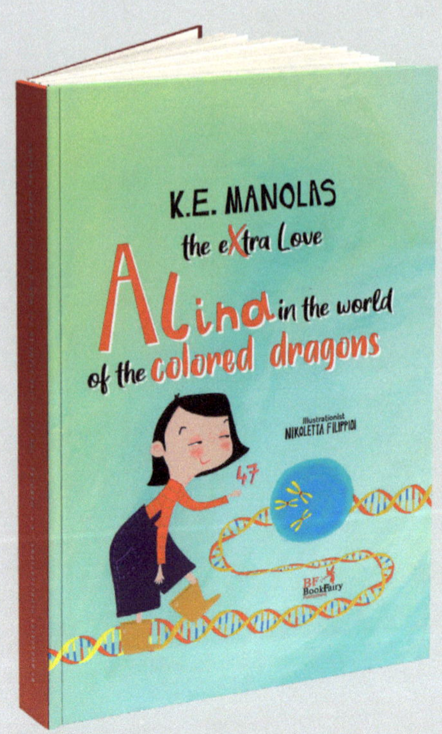